THE SALEM WITCH TRIALS

A HISTORY PERSPECTIVES BOOK

Kristin Marciniak

Published in the United States of America by Cherry Lake Publishing
Ann Arbor, Michigan
www.cherrylakepublishing.com

Consultants: Bridget M. Marshall, PhD, Associate Professor, Department of
English, University of Massachusetts, Lowell; Marla Conn, ReadAbility, Inc.
Editorial direction: Red Line Editorial
Book design and illustration: Sleeping Bear Press

Photo Credits: Library of Congress, cover (left), 1 (left), 4; Joseph E. Baker/
Library of Congress, cover (middle), 1 (middle), 14; Tompkins Harrison
Matteson/Library of Congress, cover (right), 1 (right), 22, 30; North Wind/
North Wind Picture Archives, 6, 8, 12, 16, 20, 24, 27; Peter Pelham/Library
of Congress, 19

Library of Congress Cataloging-in-Publication Data

Marciniak, Kristin.
  The Salem witch trials / Kristin Marciniak.
    pages cm. -- (Perspectives library)
  ISBN 978-1-62431-667-8 (hardcover) -- ISBN 978-1-62431-694-4 (pbk.)
-- ISBN 978-1-62431-721-7 (pdf) -- ISBN 978-1-62431-748-4 (hosted
ebook)
  1. Trials (Witchcraft)--Massachusetts--Salem--Juvenile literature. I. Title.

  KFM2478.8.W5M35 2013
  345.744'50288--dc23
                          2013029377

Cherry Lake Publishing would like to acknowledge the work of
The Partnership for 21st Century Skills. Please visit www.p21.org
for more information.

Printed in the United States of America
Corporate Graphics Inc.
January 2014

TABLE OF CONTENTS

In this book, you will read about the Salem witch trials from three perspectives. Each perspective is based on real things that happened to real people who lived in or near Salem Village in 1692. As you'll see, the same event can look different depending on one's point of view.

John Barrowe

Minister

Evil lurks among us. The first signs of the Devil's work appeared in Salem Village just a few months ago, in late January 1692. Salem Village is in Massachusetts Bay Colony. The village is only three miles from where I live in Salem Town, but the two places could not be more different. Salem Village is a rural community of 600 people and even more livestock.

Salem Town is a city formed around a large seaport. A report of the evil that began in Salem Village quickly found its way to my door.

I received an urgent letter from the minister of Salem Village in early February. Reverend Samuel Parris had been the pastor of the Salem Village church for just three years. His letter was brief. He wrote that a terrible illness had fallen upon his house. He begged me to provide my opinion on the matter.

Reverend Parris's house was in an uproar when I arrived. His nine-year-old daughter, Betty, and his 11-year-old niece, Abigail Williams, were both **afflicted** with uncontrollable fits. The girls screamed as their bodies twisted into impossible positions. They complained of bites and pinches on their arms and legs.

I asked Reverend Parris if he had sent for a doctor. He said he had. The doctor said there was nothing he could do. The doctor had not found any physical cause for the girls' distress. He believed the problem

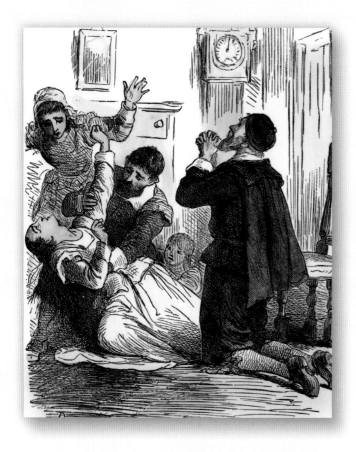

◀ *Clergy members prayed for the afflicted girls.*

was spiritual in nature, caused by demons or other evil beings. But where had it come from?

The girls eventually calmed enough to answer that question for me. Reverend Parris owns two slaves, Tituba and John Indian. According to Betty and Abigail, one afternoon at the end of January, Tituba was going to predict the future for Betty, Abigail, and some of their friends. Betty and Abigail reported that Tituba created a homemade crystal ball by dropping an egg white into a glass of water. As the egg white sank into the water, one of Betty's friends saw the outline of a coffin in the glass. All the girls immediately went into **hysterics**. Betty and Abigail had been afflicted ever since.

Fortune-telling is a crime and a sin in our culture. Only God has the right to predict future events. We believed the young girls instead of Tituba, a slave. She must have been under the influence of satanic powers. Whether she meant to harm the girls or not, her actions brought disease and despair to this community. Tituba is a witch.

We are not immune to witchcraft in the colonies. For centuries, the Devil has used witches to spread disease and suffering, hoping to destroy the Kingdom of God. We believe illnesses and events that cannot be explained—sudden blindness, the death of an infant, a failing crop—can be signs of the Devil's work.

SECOND SOURCE

▶ Find another source that describes the illnesses of Reverend Parris's daughter and niece. Compare the information there to the information in this chapter.

Until now, witchcraft in the colonies has been somewhat rare. While several witches have been accused, it wasn't until 1647 that the first witch was hanged for her crimes. There have been only a handful of **convictions** since. I suspect there will be more to come.

▲ *The girls' story implied that Tituba was a witch.*

Tituba is not the only accused witch in Salem Village. Five other girls in the village came forward shortly after I visited Reverend Parris's home. They complained of the same pains, had unexplainable fits, and spoke of seeing bright lights, small animals, and people without faces. By the end of February, three people had been named as witches. Tituba was the

TEST FOR THE BEWITCHED

Some people in Salem Village used "witch cake" to determine whether a person was under the influence of a witch. Barley meal was mixed with urine from the afflicted person. The dough was shaped into a small cake and baked. Then it was fed to a dog. If the dog acted strangely, then the person who provided the urine was bewitched. But Reverend Parris and others believed this type of test was witchcraft too.

first. Two other women in town, Sarah Good and Sarah Osborne, were also accused.

The trials began in June. People from far and wide came to watch the proceedings, myself included. The accused were questioned, and then witnesses came forward to **testify** against them. The afflicted girls, overcome with pain and sometimes suffering from deafness or violent fits, were often unable to testify. They remained in the courtroom though, and the sight of these young women thrashing about and screaming words of nonsense was deeply disturbing.

Sarah Good and Sarah Osborne denied the charges of witchcraft, but Tituba confessed that the Devil had come to her and forced her to work for him. Furthermore, Tituba claimed that she was in a **coven** with both Sarah Good and Sarah Osborne. All three women were sent to jail.

I had hoped that the matter would be put to rest once the three women had been found guilty. Instead, the afflicted continued to name even more witches. Local religious leaders gathered to discuss a way to end the afflicted girls' suffering. Disease is often a punishment from God for sins we have committed. So those in Salem Village decided to do a village-wide fast to make amends for their sins. During the fast, villagers stayed in their homes and refrained from working and eating. If these sacrifices were pleasing to God, the punishment would end. The fast lasted for ten days. It did not work.

THINK ABOUT IT

▶ Determine the main point of this paragraph. Pick out one piece of evidence that supports your answer.

More and more people are joining the ranks of the afflicted in the courtroom, and the accusations of witchcraft are coming quickly now. I once watched in horror as girls ripped at their hair and beat their chests. Now I worry about those who have been accused. Just last week, Rebecca

Nurse, a most valued member of the Salem Village church, was convicted of witchcraft. Many people signed a petition stating she was innocent. The jury first found her to be innocent, but the judges asked

▲ *Accusations of witchcraft came at an increasingly fast pace.*

them to reconsider. They found her guilty, and Sister Nurse was sentenced to death.

I find it hard to believe that such a good woman could be an instrument of the Devil's work. Reverend Parris made it clear to his congregation that anyone can be overcome by satanic forces, even the religious. But the evidence brought against Sister Nurse included only the shrieks of her accusers and their tales of **spectral** visions. I am of the mind that such spectral evidence should not be given credit, but I shall keep that to myself. Those who side with the accused often find themselves on trial as well.

Patience Dod

Accused Witch

Bridget Bishop and Sarah Good are dead. Rebecca Nurse, Elizabeth Howe, George Jacobs, and John Proctor are dead too. They were hanged in front of the rest of the town. It is the end of September 1692. Since the trials began in June, 19 people have been convicted of witchcraft and sent to the **gallows**. Will I be next?

I am not a witch. I know that for certain. I have never spoken with the Devil and never tried to harm another soul. Yet here I am, wearing leg irons and in prison until my trial. Every day, more men and women file into this overcrowded, filthy jail. The only ones who leave are headed to the gallows.

I came to prison shortly after Ann Putnam Jr. accused my older sister, Mary, of being a witch. Ann is a vile 12-year-old girl. She has accused no fewer than 68 people of serving the Devil. She makes it sound as if witches line up outside her door just for the chance to curse her.

Ann and her friends, a gang of spiteful girls all "afflicted" in one way or another, taunted my dear sister throughout her trial. They interrupted her testimony with shrieks and seizures, calling for her **specter** to stop tormenting them.

Those on trial are not allowed many rights. They cannot have legal defenders, nor are they allowed to have witnesses testify on their behalf. But they can question their accusers. Mary called Ann up to question her. The young girl was suddenly struck dumb. It was as if she could no longer see, hear, or speak. My sister, concerned about the girl, reached out and touched her shoulder. "Witch!" Ann cried, suddenly coming back to life. "Mary Dod is a witch!"

▲ *Even young children accused people of witchcraft.*

A loud murmur filled the room. I could not let my sister go undefended. I fought my way to the front of the courtroom. I said there was a guilty party in the room, but it was not my sister. Ann fell to the floor. Her body quaked as she moaned in pain. "Witch!" another of the afflicted girls cried. "I saw Patience Dod's specter attack poor Ann!" My arms were seized by two guards. I was dragged to jail, where I have been for about two months.

I now understand why so many men testify against their wives. Defending a loved one against accusations of witchcraft only makes you an easy target for the afflicted girls. I am not the first or last person who attended a trial as a **spectator** and left as a prisoner.

There are 100 people here in the Salem Village jail.

ANALYZE THIS

▶ Analyze the accounts of John Barrowe and Patience Dod. How are they different? How are they similar?

Our cramped quarters are cold and dark, and the lack of windows makes my small cell feel like a dungeon. The air stinks of human waste and tobacco. It is difficult to find an appetite for the small amount of food and water we are given. Four people have died from the horrible conditions.

THE MATHERS

Two notable clergymen gave guidance during the 1692 witchcraft crisis. Both Harvard University president Increase Mather and his son, Cotton, publicly supported the trials. But Increase did not think testimonies about dreams and visions should be allowed in the courtroom. In October 1692, Increase wrote, "It were better that ten suspected witches should escape than one innocent person be condemned."

▲ *Cotton Mather was a clergyman who thought spectral visions should not be used as evidence.*

....

Jail is expensive. We are charged for every day spent here. Beddings and food are extra. We are even forced to pay for our leg irons. I worry about what Mary and I will do if we manage to escape the gallows. We have no money to pay our prison bill. The sheriff will most likely take our meager possessions and maybe even our home. We will be left with nothing.

I must find a way to save myself and my sister. Proclaiming our innocence does nothing to sway

◀ *Those found guilty of being witches were put to death.*

....

the judges—every single person who has been hanged so far has claimed their innocence until the very end. If I refuse to take part in the trial, that will not help either. Giles Corey would not answer any of the judge's questions. They pressed him to death with heavy stones.

The only ones who live are those who admit to witchcraft. Many of them, like Tituba, have gone to court to testify against others. They remain in jail between trials. While they aren't free, they are still alive.

I know I have been falsely accused. The same must be true for at least some of the others, yet they

20

have taken blame in order to survive. Should I lie, like I suspect Tituba did, and say that I am a witch to save my own neck? Or should I, like the 19 already hanged, declare my innocence as the heavy rope tightens around my neck?

I do not have much time to decide. There are murmurs of unease in our village and the surrounding towns. People are getting angry about the executions. I am not sure how the judges will react. Will they kill us all to rid the town of the Devil? Or will we be released and left to pick up the pieces of our lives?

SECOND SOURCE

▶ Find another source that documents what happened in the courtroom during the Salem witch trials. Compare the information there to the information in this chapter.

3

Martha Smart

Accuser

The entire town thought I was bewitched. Looking back, I don't think I was. I was 14 years old in 1692. My parents had just died from illnesses, so my uncle took me in. I was treated like a servant. I cleaned, cooked, fed the pigs, and watched my young cousins. My uncle was not a wealthy man, and he already had four children of his own. I was a **burden** to him and my aunt, and they mostly ignored me. It was an unpleasant life, but it was the lot I had been dealt.

I became ill with a fever and terrible stomach pains in January 1692. When the fever was at its worst, I had visions of a tall, thin black man beckoning me to follow him. I was terrified to tell my uncle for fear that he'd accuse me of making up stories and throw me out of the house. I suffered alone until my cousin brought news from the village. Other girls had the same stomach pains and fever from which I ailed. There were even hushed whispers about visions just like mine. Doctors said these symptoms were caused by witchcraft.

My uncle thought otherwise. He said my illness was a punishment for my sins. The only way I would return to health was to go to church.

I'll never forget the events of one Sunday. My fever had cooled and I looked forward to the sermon. Halfway through the service, Betty Parris's cousin Abigail stood up and began naming people who had bewitched her.

The accused were taken to jail while other girls added their voices to Abigail's. They clawed at their skin, moaning that they were being tortured by the accused people's specters.

The entire congregation was **riveted** by the scene. When the girls' fits ended, both relatives and strangers rushed to their sides. They comforted the afflicted girls and vowed to punish those responsible.

I fell into a deep sleep when we returned to the house. Hours later, I woke screaming, plagued by nightmares of the tall black man. My cousin rushed into the room, but she could not comfort me.

◀ *Several girls in Salem Village accused community members of witchcraft.*

My uncle joined us. I was babbling, making very little sense. My uncle looked into my eyes with the care of a father. How I had longed for such attention from him! He asked what demon had bewitched me. I named the first person who came to my mind: Sarah Good.

Sarah Good was well known in Salem Village for all the wrong reasons. She was a homeless beggar who smoked a pipe and was rude to people who offered her charity. I had never spoken to her in my life.

My uncle thundered from the house in search of Reverend Parris while my aunt and cousin helped me into bed. I had never before known such tender care and affection. My chores were put on hold day after day while doctors and ministers visited my bedside to ask about my visions and how I was feeling. They listened to my every word.

THINK ABOUT IT

▶ Determine the main point of this page. Pick out one piece of evidence that supports your answer.

I began to feel better over the next few weeks, but I didn't want the attention to stop. I continued to complain of aches and **hallucinations** while my aunt held my hand and prayed. I didn't like lying, but the thought of suddenly losing their affection was more than I could bear.

The trials began in early June. I was completely recovered by this time, but a group of village elders convinced my uncle that I should attend the proceedings with the rest of the afflicted girls.

Ann Putnam Jr. was the ringleader in the courtroom. I was unsure how to act, so I followed her lead. We made fun of the accused by mimicking their actions. We screamed and flailed our limbs.

People were listening to us for the first time in our lives. What we said actually mattered. The power was thrilling, but things were spiraling out of control.

The hangings started on June 10. Bridget Bishop was the first. She owned a tavern and never had anything nice to say about anyone. Her death cleared the way for more and more outcasts to be accused, convicted, and sent to jail. One by one, they were dragged to the gallows in a wooden cart and put to death.

It all happened so quickly. It felt like the adults were pushing us to accuse more people. A sense of hysteria filled the village and spread to outlying towns. Nobody knew whom to trust. I no longer wanted to

▲ *The accusers often thrashed around in the courtroom.*

be a part of this, but it was too late. I had to continue. If my lies had been discovered, I would have been severely punished.

Thankfully, Governor William Phips stepped in before we could do any more damage. He stopped the trials on October 29, 1692. Some people say it was because the townspeople were so upset by the number of convictions and accusations. I think it was because his wife was accused of being a witch. Whatever the reason, I was glad it was over.

Those still in jail under suspicion of witchcraft were tried in January 1693 in a new court in Boston. Unlike the earlier trials, spectral evidence was not allowed in the courtroom. Only a few people were convicted, but they were eventually released with everyone else in May 1693.

ANALYZE THIS

▶ Analyze the accounts of Patience Dod and Martha Smart. How are their stories alike? How are they different?

It has been ten years since the end of the trials. Witchcraft no longer takes the blame for accidents and diseases here in Salem Village. No apology will ever undo the damage wrought in 1692. What I did in Salem Village all those years ago cannot be excused, but I hope it can be understood.

WHAT REALLY HAPPENED?

Nobody knows exactly what caused the wave of witchcraft accusations in Salem Village. Some historians think it was due to a disease called encephalitis. Encephalitis can cause pricking sensations, fits, and hallucinations. Others say the Indian Wars were to blame. Several of the accusers lost their families in these bloody battles and blamed others for the Puritans' failure. And some scholars blame the accusers of pretending to be ill to get attention.

LOOK, LOOK AGAIN

Take a close look at this illustration of a witch trial and answer the following questions:

1. How would a member of the clergy react to the events taking place in this picture? Would he side with the accused or the afflicted? Why?

2. How would an accused witch describe this picture? What thoughts would he or she have when looking at this scene?

3. What would an accuser think when she saw this picture? How would her reaction be different from that of the accused?

GLOSSARY

afflicted (uh-FLIK-ted) suffering or troubled

burden (BUR-duhn) a heavy load or responsibility

convictions (kuhn-VIK-shuhns) formal declarations that people have committed crimes

coven (KUH-vin) a group of witches

gallows (GAL-ohz) a structure used for hanging criminals

hallucinations (huh-LOO-suh-nae-shuhns) objects believed to be seen but that are not real

hysterics (his-TER-iks) fits of uncontrollable laughter or crying

riveted (RIV-ih-ted) having one's attention held completely

spectator (SPEK-tay-tur) a person who watches an event but does not participate

specter (SPEK-tur) a ghost or spirit

spectral (SPEK-trul) relating to spirits or visions and dreams

testify (TES-tuh-fye) to make a formal statement in a court of law about what one knows or has witnessed

LEARN MORE

Further Reading

Dolan, Edward F. *The Salem Witch Trials*. New York: Benchmark Books, 2002.
Orr, Tamra. *The Salem Witch Trials*. San Diego, CA: Blackbirch, 2004.
Schanzer, Rosalyn. *Witches! The Absolutely True Tale of Disaster in Salem*. Washington, DC: National Geographic Society, 2011.

Web Sites

Salem Witchcraft Hysteria
http://www.nationalgeographic.com/features/97/salem/
This interactive Web site allows readers to experience the Salem witch trials as if they were there.

The Salem Witchcraft Site
http://www.tulane.edu/~salem/index.html
Visitors to this Web site will read lots of data and interpretations of what happened during the Salem witch trials.

INDEX

ABOUT THE AUTHOR

Kristin Marciniak writes the books she wishes she had read in school. Her journalism degree from the University of Missouri–Columbia comes in handy when she writes about the Navy SEALs, the flu pandemic of 1918, and other exciting times in U.S. history. Marciniak lives in Kansas City, Missouri, with her husband and son.